Provinces and Territories of Canada

MANITOBA

— *"Spirited Energy"* —

Published by Weigl Educational Publishers Limited
6325 10 Street SE
Calgary, Alberta
T2H 2Z9

www.weigl.com

Library and Archives Canada Cataloguing in Publication data available upon request.
Fax 403-233-7769 for the attention of the Publishing Records department.

ISBN 978-1-55388-974-8 (hard cover)
ISBN 978-1-55388-987-8 (soft cover)

Printed in the United States of America
1 2 3 4 5 6 7 8 9 0 13 12 11 10 09

Editor: Heather C. Hudak
Design: Terry Paulhus

All of the Internet URLs given in the book were valid at the time of publication. However, due to the dynamic nature of the Internet,
some addresses may have changed, or sites may have ceased to exist since publication. While the author and publisher regret any
inconvenience this may cause readers, no responsibility for any such changes can be accepted by either the author or the publisher.

Every reasonable effort has been made to trace ownership and to obtain permission to reprint copyright material. The publishers
would be pleased to have any errors or omissions brought to their attention so that they may be corrected in subsequent printings.

Weigl acknowledges Getty Images as its primary image supplier for this title.
Festival du Voyageur: page 32; Gimli Icelandic Festival: page 33 top; Glenbow Archives: page 27 top; Hudson Bay Company Archives,
Provincial Archives of Manitoba: pages 24, 26, 27 bottom, 30; Inco Limited: page: 10 top; National Archives of Canada: pages 26 top,
31 right; Provincial Archives of Manitoba: page 31 left; Winnipeg Fringe Theatre Festival: page 38.

We gratefully acknowledge the financial support of the Government of Canada through the Book Publishing Industry Development
Program (BPIDP) for our publishing activities.

Contents

Manitoba

Although Manitoba is known for its treeless prairies and fertile farmland, its natural scenery extends beyond flat landscapes. Rocky terrains, small mountains, and dense forest regions can all be found in the province. Together with Alberta and Saskatchewan, Manitoba is one of the three Prairie Provinces. As the easternmost of the Prairie Provinces, Manitoba is known as Canada's Keystone Province. A keystone is the stone at the top of an arch that balances the weight of both sides, keeping the arch in place. Manitoba balances eastern and western Canada. It lies in the centre of the country, a transportation **junction** between the industrial centres of the east and the prairies and mountains of the West.

Winnipeg is the capital of Manitoba. It is the oldest city on the Prairies.

Lake Winnipeg has an area of 24,514 square kilometres, making it the 13th largest lake in the world.

Manitoba has about 100,000 lakes that are the remains of a huge body of water. Known as Lake Agassiz, it covered the southern region after the Ice Age. Today, Manitoba's largest lakes are Lake Winnipeg, Lake Winnipegosis, and Lake Manitoba. Rivers in Manitoba include the Saskatchewan, Red, Nelson, Churchill, and Assiniboine Rivers and their **tributaries**. A part of northern Manitoba runs along the shore of Hudson Bay. About 25 percent of North America's fresh water drains through Manitoba's rivers into Hudson Bay. Although it is in the heart of Canada, Manitoba has more than 600 kilometres of saltwater coastline.

The name Manitoba probably comes from the Algonquian words "Manitou bau," which means "Strait of the Spirit," or "Narrows of the Great Spirit." The name refers to a narrow part of Lake Manitoba. When the lake's waves break on the loose surface rocks of the north shore, they make an odd wailing sound. Early Aboriginal Peoples thought this was the sound of the Great Spirit Manitou beating on a huge drum.

Manitoba's southern region is a major contributor to Canada's breadbasket. Vast harvests of wheat, barley, oats, and flax come out of the region.

In winter, the province's frozen lakes can be used as roads to bring goods to the isolated northern communities.

Manitoba has a number of unique cities and communities. Winnipeg is the largest city in the province and is located at the junction of the Red and Assiniboine Rivers. It is the centre of road, rail, and river networks. Winnipeg is 16 times as big as the next largest Manitoba city, Brandon. Brandon is nicknamed the "Wheat City" because of its strong agricultural heritage and successful farming communities. Other Manitoba communities include Portage-la-Prairie, which lies west of Winnipeg, Flin Flon, which lies northwest of Winnipeg, and Thompson, in the far north. Churchill is even farther north, nestled on the shores of the Hudson Bay.

GET THE FACTS

Bass, pickerel, pike, sauger, trout, and whitefish are plentiful in Manitoba's lakes and rivers.

Manitoba has 127 provincial parks, nine natural parks, one wilderness park, 31 recreation parks, and many national history parks.

Manitoba's Riding Mountain National Park encompasses vast areas of aspen parkland, deciduous forest, and open grasslands and meadows.

LAND AND CLIMATE

Mount Baldy, in the Duck Mountains, is the province's highest point.

Manitoba's southern region consists of plains with rolling grasslands and few trees. However, prairie does not dominate the entire Manitoba landscape. North of Winnipeg, the prairie gives way to sparkling lakes and dense forests.

The **Canadian Shield** is another feature of Manitoba's landscape. It makes up about two-thirds of the province's northern region, and consists mainly of low hills, forests, lakes, and a plateau of soft rock from ancient mountains. The large, ancient rocks of the Canadian Shield are often marked with coloured streaks and deposits of minerals. Some of these rocks are almost as old as the Earth itself.

Most of the land in Manitoba is very flat, and flooding and erosion are always a threat. Many farmers have planted trees around their properties to act as windbreaks. They have also dug irrigation ditches to funnel away floodwaters.

Gravel beaches and sandy delta areas on the Manitoba plains show the former shoreline of Lake Agassiz.

To the far north, stretching about 160 kilometres inland from Hudson Bay, is the Hudson Bay Lowland. It is a cold, treeless area of **tundra**.

There is a hilly region in the southwest of Manitoba. Highlands in this region are called the Porcupine Hills, the Duck Mountains, and the Turtle Mountains. The Turtle Mountains are the lowest mountain range in North America.

Warm, moist ocean winds do not reach Manitoba because it is 2,000 kilometres from the Pacific Ocean. The province's location results in long, cold winters, and warm, short summers.

The climate is quite dry, and most precipitation falls in the summer as short bursts of rain. Snowfall in Manitoba is not heavy, but due to the cold winter temperatures, snow stays on the ground from November to April.

NATURAL RESOURCES

Smelting involves melting ore in order to obtain metal. A smelter in Thompson produces nickel.

Manitoba's waters are an important resource. Not only are they well suited to recreational activities, they also contain fish that support both commercial and sport fishing.

The province's swift-flowing rivers are excellent for the production of **hydroelectric** power. The production is so efficient that Manitoba provides more electricity than it needs from its hydroelectric power plants. The province's extra hydroelectric power is sold to other provinces.

(i) KEEP CONNECTED

The Manitoba Hydro website has a great deal of information about energy sources. For interactive games and activities, visit **www.hydro.mb.ca/learning_zone/index.shtml.**

One of Manitoba's most valuable resources is its fertile prairie land. About 7.6 million hectares of this land are used for farming.

Manitoba also has many useful minerals. The Canadian Shield contains large amounts of metallic ores. The most important is nickel, which makes up 30 percent of the value of all the minerals mined in the province. All the nickel is produced in the northern city of Thompson.

Flin Flon is the oldest of the mining centres and produces copper, zinc, and small amounts of gold and silver. Precious metals have also been found at centres such as Lynn Lake and Leaf Rapids. Petroleum is another important natural resource in Manitoba. It is found in the area of Virden, in the southwest region of the province.

GET THE FACTS

The city of Flin Flon may have been named for Professor Josiah Flintabbatey Flonatin, a character in a science fiction novel titled *The Sunless City* by E. Preston Muddock.

Half of Manitoba is covered with non-productive forest. This means the trees are not suitable for the lumber industry.

PLANTS AND ANIMALS

The white spruce is the provincial tree of Manitoba.

The prairie crocus is the provincial flower of Manitoba.

The vegetation in Manitoba is diverse. Tall, mixed grass species make up most of the southern prairie area. Willows, aspens, and poplars grow in the moist river valleys, and some oaks grow in dry spots.

From spring to fall, wildflowers appear among the grasses. Farther north, there are regions of open prairie with stands of aspen, birch, and poplar. Still farther north, the forests are a mixture of **coniferous** and **deciduous** trees. There are also colourful chokecherry, cranberry, and saskatoon bushes in Manitoba's wetlands.

Near Hudson Bay, the land is barren and treeless, with a few grasses and wildflowers among the mosses and lichens. Roots are very shallow because the ground is always frozen.

In the tundra, where the climate is extreme, lichens and mosses cover the ground. Spruce, willows, and bearberry bushes occasionally dot the landscape.

Manitoba is home to three types of caribou. These are coastal, barren ground, and boreal woodland.

Manitoba has an abundance of interesting wildlife. A very large community of polar bears live near Churchill. Every once in a while, a polar bear will wander into the town attracted by the food in the local garbage dumps.

Manitoba's Hudson Bay area also hosts beluga whales. In the summer, hundreds of these whales gather at the mouth of the Churchill River to feed.

The southern forests are home to moose, caribou, elk, and deer. Black bears, beavers, and other small fur-bearing animals also live in these forests.

Today, there are about 25,000 polar bears in the world. A large number of them can be found in the far north of Manitoba.

The great grey owl is the provincial bird. It likes to make its home in empty nests in aspen swamps.

Wolverines and white and blue foxes live on the tundra, while caribou, wolves, otters, lynx, squirrels, and mink are found in the far north. Coyotes and badgers like Manitoba's open country.

Many types of birds are found in Manitoba. Grouse, wild turkeys, and prairie chickens are common. There are also ducks and geese on the ponds and swamps of the province. Bald eagles are occasionally spotted.

Lynxes inhabit Manitoba's northern forests.

TOURISM

The Royal Canadian Mint, in Winnipeg, makes two billion coins each year for Canada and many other nations. Thousands of tourists take tours of the factory and museum.

Manitoba attracts many wildlife enthusiasts. About 10,000 tourists a year take a ride on a "tundra buggy" from Churchill to watch the polar bears. Other tourists may ride on a **hydrophone**-equipped boat to see and hear the belugas that swim in the area. Close to Churchill, the Tundra Aurora Domes are areas with 360° views from which people can watch the northern lights.

Winnipeg is home to The Forks, a huge riverside area that offers recreational and cultural events to visitors all year round. At the junction of the Red and Assiniboine Rivers, The Forks is a location

The Forks is one of Winnipeg's most popular gathering places. The market there offers jewellery, crafts, and a variety of fresh and specialty foods.

16 PROVINCES AND TERRITORIES OF CANADA

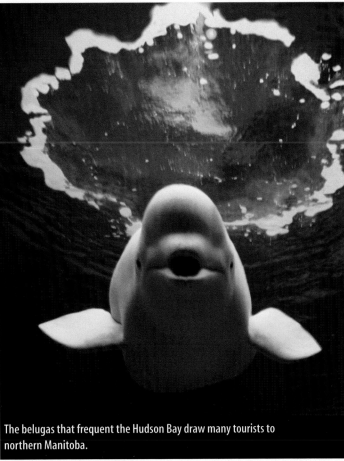

The belugas that frequent the Hudson Bay draw many tourists to northern Manitoba.

for concerts, children's programs, historical exhibitions, and shopping. Visitors can hike, ice-skate, or cross-country ski there.

The Manitoba Museum in Winnipeg has several life-size exhibits that show the province's natural and cultural heritage. The Boreal Forest Gallery, for example, depicts Manitoba's most northerly forested region. Other exhibits include pioneer life, a buffalo hunt, and a 1920s Winnipeg street.

GET THE FACTS

Lower Fort Garry National Historic Site, at Selkirk, still has many of the original buildings from the 1830s Hudson's Bay Company trading post.

Prairie Dog Central is a steam-driven train that takes tourists on a two-hour, round-trip from Winnipeg to Grosse-Isle.

Grand Beach Provincial Park has white sand beaches that attract many tourists.

The Commonwealth Air Training Plan Museum, in Brandon, is dedicated to the soldiers who fought in the Commonwealth during World War II. It has over 5,000 displays of aircraft memorabilia and artifacts for visitors to enjoy.

The swinging bridge in Souris is 177 metres long. It is the longest swinging bridge in Canada.

Manitoba is responsible for about 12 to 15 percent of Canada's total wheat production each year.

Agriculture is one of Manitoba's most important industries. It is the main economic activity for most of the rural communities in southern Manitoba. Agriculture is confined to the south of the province because the growing season in the north is too short and the soil is poor. The major crop is wheat. Other significant crops include canola, flaxseed, and barley. Ranching also contributes to the economy.

Manitoba is a vital centre for trade. Winnipeg is one of Canada's leading grain markets. It also trades cattle and serves as a major distribution centre for farm and factory products.

Nearly one fifth of Manitoba's wealth comes from financial services, real estate sales, and insurance.

Manufacturing is important in Manitoba. Processed food, transportation equipment, machinery, and printed products are all manufactured in the province. The most important centre for manufacturing is Winnipeg because of its large supply of inexpensive electricity and its convenient, central location.

GET THE FACTS

Most of the trees cut in Manitoba are small and are used either to make wood pulp or to build furniture.

The commercial fishing industry is centred on Manitoba's three major lakes and Hudson Bay. Most of the province's fish is exported to the United States.

GOODS AND SERVICES

Manitoba's railway maintenance facilities and marshalling yards provide many jobs for people in the province.

Churchill is home to one of the few commercial shipping ports on the shore of the Hudson Bay.

Winnipeg is central to Manitoba's and Canada's railway network. It has often been regarded as the "Gateway to the West" because of its central location within Canada. To service the engines and train cars, the city has extensive marshalling yards and repair facilities.

The railway is the most important way of moving goods from Manitoba to other places. Grain is transported by rail to the Atlantic and Pacific Oceans and to the port of Churchill on the Hudson Bay. The railway also carries aviation and marine fuels to the Hudson Bay area and minerals from the mines in the Canadian Shield region.

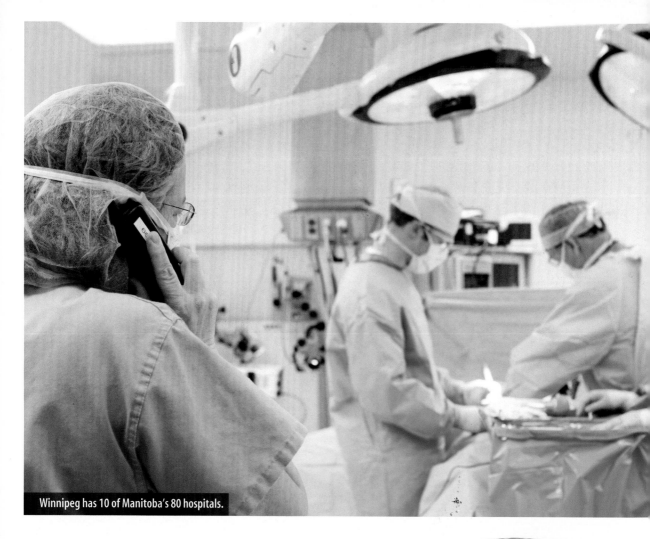

Winnipeg has 10 of Manitoba's 80 hospitals.

Most highways connect through Winnipeg. Since it is a traffic junction, it is a suitable marketplace for grain, cattle, and farm produce from the Prairies. Many farmers around Winnipeg produce vegetables and dairy goods to sell in the city.

Winnipeg is the centre of education in the province. The University of Manitoba, which is in Winnipeg, is one of the biggest universities in Canada. The university was established in 1877, making it the first university in western Canada. Manitoba has three other universities as well. These are the University of Winnipeg, Brandon University, and the Canadian Mennonite University.

Manitoba had the first publicly owned telephone system in North America.

Five television stations and 27 radio stations serve the province.

Community colleges in many Manitoba towns and cities offer training in trades and technologies. Saint Boniface College is located in Winnipeg's French-speaking community of Saint Boniface. The college uses French as its language of instruction.

GET THE FACTS

Railway and trucking firms make up the most important part of Manitoba's transportation industry.

The shortest route to Europe is via Hudson Bay, but it is not used in winter when the bay is iced over. The alternative route is through the Great Lakes.

There are five daily newspapers in the province and more than 78 weekly or bi-weekly newspapers, including *La Liberté*, which is written in French.

The Yellowhead Highway, which passes through Manitoba, roughly follows a part of the Ellice Trail, an old fur-trading route.

FIRST NATIONS

Aboriginal groups in the Manitoba region often ended up sharing some hunting and fishing grounds. Sometimes, competition for food and land led to confrontations.

Most historians agree that the first inhabitants arrived in the Manitoba region about 11,000 or 12,000 years ago. These inhabitants were probably hunters who were following the buffalo. Later, Aboriginal Peoples began hunting in the northern forests.

Early Inuit were on the shores of Hudson Bay about 3,000 years ago. By the early seventeenth century, five Aboriginal groups occupied the Manitoba region. The Inuit lived in the far north, along the Hudson Bay. They hunted whales in the bay and caribou in the forest. Also in the North were the Chipewyans, who competed with the Inuit in hunting for caribou. The Inuit and Chipewyan were natural enemies.

KEEP CONNECTED

Hunting bison was an essential part of the Assiniboine's economy and culture. Learn more about the Assiniboine at www.thecanadianencyclopedia.com. Type "Assiniboine" into the search engine, and click on the first article.

Thousands of years ago, Aboriginal Peoples may have hunted woolly mammoths in the region.

Within 100 years, from the late 1700s to 1890, the Assiniboine population decreased from around 10,000 to 2,600. Many died of smallpox—a disease brought by European explorers and settlers.

The Woodland Cree lived just south of the Inuit and the Chipewyans. This group hunted in the region's rich forest and fished in its rivers. The Plains Cree fished and trapped animals in the prairies and lowlands of Manitoba. The Ojibwa, who were closely related to the Cree, dominated the central Manitoba region. Finally, the Assiniboine lived in the southern region. The Assiniboine and Cree were close allies.

EXPLORERS

Henry Kelsey is famous for exploring the Canadian plains between 1690 and 1692.

The first European to set foot in the Manitoba region was Captain Thomas Button. He spent the winter of 1612 on the shore of Hudson Bay near the mouths of the Nelson and Hayes Rivers. Button claimed the land for Britain. It was many years before other explorers arrived.

In the late 1600s, explorers came looking for furs. The Hudson's Bay Company, a British fur-trading company, built its main post at York Factory on the Hayes River. One of the company's agents, Henry Kelsey, spent three years exploring the area extending from the tundra south to the Saskatchewan River.

In the 1730s, a French explorer named Pierre Gaultier de La Vérendrye led an expedition west from the Great Lakes. He explored the Red River Valley and built four forts. More French explorers soon followed to set up further posts.

Beaver fur was a much-desired catch for fur traders in the 1700s. Hats made from beaver fur were quite fashionable in England at the time.

Many French fur traders married Cree and Ojibwa women. Their children were called Métis.

Unlicensed French, Scottish, and American trappers also began to operate. The Hudson's Bay Company had always waited for trappers to bring their furs north to them. Now, because of the new competition, the company had to start building posts closer to the traders.

GET THE FACTS

La Vérendrye's trading headquarters were at Fort La Reine, near present-day Portage-la-Prairie.

Thousands of Aboriginal Peoples died when Europeans brought diseases such as smallpox to the area.

The Métis learned the skills of both the Europeans and Aboriginal Peoples. They were able to help the Europeans survive in harsh conditions.

The English and French competed for control of the fur trade.

Aboriginal Peoples worked as trappers, guides, and interpreters in the fur trade.

The Hudson's Bay Company set up fur-trading posts across the country.

During the early 1800s, the Hudson's Bay Company was fighting with the North West Company of Montreal for control of the fur trade. Both companies built forts across the plains and even fought battles in the Red River and Assiniboine River Valleys.

In 1812, Lord Selkirk of the Hudson's Bay Company, sent a group of Scottish immigrants to set up a colony on the Red River. Members of the North West Company, who had forts in the area, saw the move as a plot to block their trading routes.

In the spring of 1816, Selkirk's men seized the North West Company's Fort Gibraltar. They were trying to stop the North West Company from exporting **pemmican**. Métis who worked for the North West Company captured the Hudson's Bay Company's Brandon House in order to reclaim the company's pemmican supplies and export them.

The Seven Oaks Incident was the worst occurrence in a long rivalry between the Hudson's Bay Company and the North West Company.

Manitoba's settlers survived many hardships before farming became established in the Red River Valley. On June 19, 1816, Governor Robert Semple led a group of settlers out to confront the Métis. What followed was the Seven Oaks Incident. The governor, 20 of Selkirk's men, and one Métis were killed. Peace was restored when the Hudson's Bay Company and the North West Company merged in 1821. Living conditions were hard during the next few years, and the settlers had to learn to live together.

The Canadian government bought the entire northwest of Canada from the Hudson's Bay Company in 1869. The Métis were angry that the deal had been done without consulting them. Led by Louis Riel, they set up their own government and fought against the transfer of the Red River Valley to Canada.

Louis Riel was the head of a provisional government that negotiated the terms of Manitoba's formation.

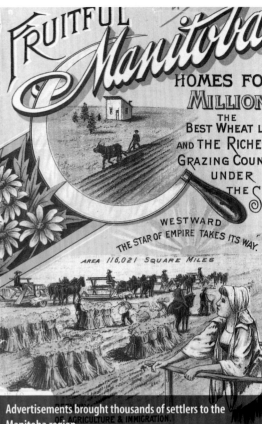

Advertisements brought thousands of settlers to the Manitoba region.

The Canadian government and the Métis reached an agreement a year later with the Manitoba Act. This act made Manitoba the fifth province of Canada and provided a Bill of Rights for the Métis. The bill included French Roman Catholic Schools for the Métis and the official use of the French language.

Manitoba's population increased rapidly after it became a province and the railroad reached the region. The fertile prairies and the demand for wheat attracted settlers from eastern Canada and immigrants from all over Europe.

GET THE FACTS

Missionaries were the first people to build schools in Manitoba. Joseph Provencher opened the first school in 1818, and John West opened another school two years later.

German-speaking Mennonites came to Manitoba from Russia, fleeing from war and violence. They set up the first Mennonite Brethren Congregation, near Winkler.

Missionaries arrived in Manitoba around the same time as the first settlers.

About 125,000 immigrants arrived from eastern Canada, Britain, and Europe between 1871 and 1891.

Manitoba has one of the largest French populations west of Quebec.

Manitoba has a population of 1.1 million. The province is made up of many cultures. People have come from all over the world to make their homes in Manitoba.

The towns and villages of the southwest, where Lord Selkirk's colonists once settled, are mainly British, while people with French ancestry live mostly south of Winnipeg.

In 1881, the Canadian Pacific Railway reached Winnipeg. Many of the Chinese workers who built the railway decided to make their home in Manitoba. Their descendants are still there today.

KEEP CONNECTED

Learn more about Manitoba's largest city—Winnipeg—by visiting www.winnipeg.caloremipsum_dolor/amet.net.

The community of Gimli, on the west shore of Lake Winnipeg, is the largest Icelandic settlement outside of Iceland.

In 1896, the government sent Clifford Sifton on a campaign to Eastern Europe to offer free land to peasant farmers. About 200,000 immigrants arrived in a period of 15 years. Icelanders set up a fishing and farming community near Gimli. Today, Gimli is a thriving Icelandic community.

After World War I, the only large wave of immigrants to arrive in Manitoba consisted of Hutterites from the United States who moved to the province in 1918. However, thousands of refugees arrived from war-torn Europe arrived after World War II.

Only 5 percent of Manitoba's population live in the northern and eastern parts of the province.

Aboriginal Peoples make up about 12 percent of Manitoba's population.

In the last 30 years, many of Manitoba's immigrants have come from the Caribbean, Central and South America, Africa, and Asia.

POLITICS AND GOVERNMENT

Manitoba became a Canadian province on July 15, 1870. When the province joined Confederation in 1870, it was a small, square area—36,000 square kilometres—surrounding the Red River Valley. The province was enlarged in 1881 and again in 1912 to its present area of 649,950 square kilometres.

In 1911, an architectural contest was held to see who could come up with the best design for the province's Legislative Building. An architect named Frank Worthington Simon won the contest, and the $10,000 prize.

The first provincial government had 24 members, 12 each from English and French districts. Today, the Legislative Assembly has 57 elected members (MLAs) in one chamber. The majority party forms the government, and its leader, the premier, chooses a Cabinet. This executive council decides on government policy and carries out the Assembly's decisions.

Municipalities are responsible for local services such as roads and sewers. Community councils, mainly Métis, give advice to the Department of Northern Affairs in the smaller northern areas. Provincial policing is provided by the Royal Canadian Mounted Police, though cities and towns employ a number of police officers to maintain law and order.

The Golden Boy stands on the top of the dome on Manitoba's **Legislative Building**.

Edward Richard Schreyer, a Manitoban, was the youngest MLA ever. He entered the legislature at the age of 22 and became premier of Manitoba at 33. He later became the governor general of Canada.

The first seven governments in Manitoba were non-partisan, meaning they had no distinct political parties.

CULTURAL GROUPS

Saint Boniface has a large Francophone community. Every February, the community honours the early fur traders at the Festival du Voyageur. Tourtière and sugar pie are dishes the voyagers would have enjoyed. These dishes are among the traditional foods served during the festival.

Manitoba has more ethnic groups than any other province. These groups are proud of their various heritages and work hard to maintain and celebrate their cultural traditions. Many of the Icelanders who settled on the southern shore of Lake Winnipeg have kept their language and customs alive. Every year, they share their culture with others at Islendingadagurinn, or the Gimli Icelandic Festival.

Many descendants of Manitoba's original Mennonite settlers have retained the old culture and traditions. The Mennonite Heritage Village in Steinbach gives visitors an idea of what an original Mennonite village looked like. Antiques, manuscripts, furnished buildings, and a **gristmill** are all part of the village.

One of Manitoba's most important festivals is Folklorama. This festival of nations takes place in Winnipeg every August and features more than 40 **pavillions** that exhibit and celebrate cultures. There, Manitoba's various cultural groups share their traditions with other Manitobans and with visitors. Traditional food, dancing, music, costumes, and crafts are all a part of the festival.

Rodeos in Manitoba celebrate the province's cattle ranching roots.

Dauphin, in southwest Manitoba, holds Canada's National Ukrainian Festival every summer.

The International Peace Garden is another source of cultural celebration. On the border with the United States, the International Peace Garden honours the relationship between Canada and the United States. The Peace Tower at the International Peace Garden has four columns representing the four corners of the world.

Every summer, students from all over North America travel there to attend an International Music Camp for band, choir, orchestra, dance, and drama.

he Red River Exhibition, eld for 10 days in une, celebrates Winnipeg's history.

The Mennonite Heritage Village has a gristmill and a windmill. Mennonites brought their knowledge of mills from countries such as Belgium, Germany, and the Netherlands.

Most of Manitoba's Aboriginal Peoples speak English, but Cree, Chipewyan, and Sioux are also heard around the province.

About 74 percent of Manitobans have English as their first language. The other major languages spoken in the province are French, German, and Ukrainian. These languages are mainly spoken in rural communities.

The Jewish community in Manitoba is very strong. It has raised millions of dollars to build the Asper Jewish Community Centre, which houses a high school, a modern fitness centre, and community groups.

ARTS AND ENTERTAINMENT

The Winnipeg Fringe Festival provides live theatre in an informal setting. It is one of the largest Fringe Festivals in North America.

Manitoba has a strong music scene, ranging from country music festivals to a highly praised symphony orchestra. Music festivals throughout the province offer great entertainment. The Winnipeg Folk Festival attracts singers and musicians from all over North America. Other festivals include The Old Time Fiddlers Contest at the International Peace Gardens, the Cripple Creek Music Festival of Bluegrass, Country, and Gospel music, the Brandon Folk Music and Art Festival, and Rockin' the Fields of Minnedosa. Manitobans have done well in rock and pop music. The Crash Test Dummies, Burton Cummings and Randy Bachman of The Guess Who, and Chantal Kreviazuk are all world-famous performers who hail from Manitoba.

Manitoba is rich in other art forms as well. The Royal Winnipeg Ballet, which was founded in 1938, is the second oldest ballet company in North America. Dancers from all over Canada work hard for the opportunity to dance with the Royal Winnipeg Ballet. It has performed all over the world.

The Winnipeg Symphony and the Winnipeg Chamber Orchestra are respected throughout Canada.

Chantal Kreviazuk is from Winnipeg. Her music is popular in Canada and around the world.

Each summer, Rainbow Stage puts on two Broadway musicals in Winnipeg's Kildonan Park. The Manitoba Theatre Centre has a main stage where it presents a series of well-known plays. Less **mainstream** productions take place on the centre's smaller stage. The Fringe Festival puts on plays and revues written mostly by Manitobans.

Many talented artists and architects are from Manitoba. Lionel Fitzgerald was a member of the famous **Group of Seven**. Walter Phillips is a Manitoban whose etchings, woodcuts, and prints are very popular. Important Manitoban architects have also made an impact on the art world. John D. Atchison designed nearly 100 of the buildings in Winnipeg, and Étienne Gaboury has designed important buildings in Saint Boniface, Mexico, and Africa.

The Winnipeg Art Gallery has a huge display of Inuit artwork.

The Cercle Molière in Saint Boniface is one of the oldest French language theatres in the country.

Two of Manitoba's best-known authors are Margaret Laurence and Gabrielle Roy. Many of their novels are about Manitoba life.

Fred Penner, a famous children's entertainer, is from Manitoba.

During the 1930s, conservation writer Grey Owl lived in Riding Mountain National Park.

The Saint Boniface Museum dates from 1846 and is the oldest building in Winnipeg. It is also the largest oak log Red River Frame building in North America.

Whiteshell Provincial Park has more than 130 lakes that are great for fishing, boating, or swimming.

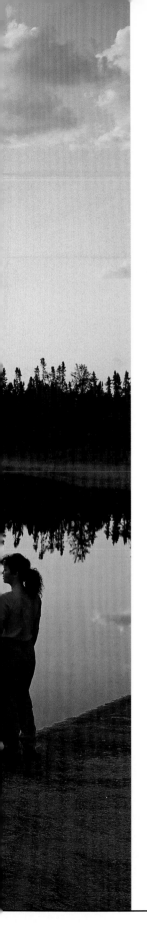

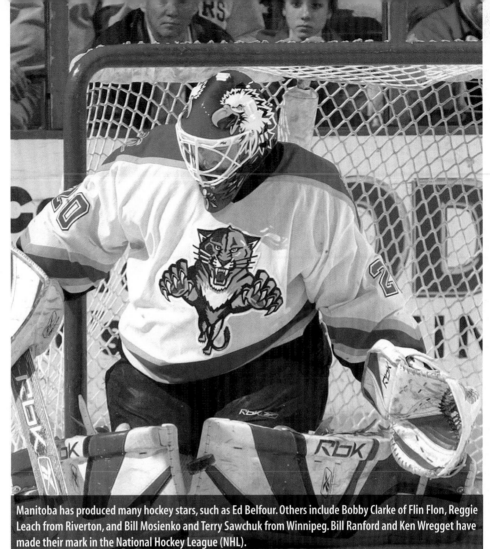

Manitoba has produced many hockey stars, such as Ed Belfour. Others include Bobby Clarke of Flin Flon, Reggie Leach from Riverton, and Bill Mosienko and Terry Sawchuk from Winnipeg. Bill Ranford and Ken Wregget have made their mark in the National Hockey League (NHL).

Sports such as hockey, ringette, and curling are all very popular in Manitoba because of its long, cold winters. There are leagues for every age group.

The Winnipeg Jets were Manitoba's professional hockey team. The Jets played in the World Hockey Association until 1979, at which time they became a part of the National Hockey League. In 1997, they moved to Phoenix, Arizona and became the Phoenix Coyotes.

Manitoba has many provincial parks that have wonderful facilities for skiers, hikers, campers, backpackers, tennis players, and lawn bowlers. Lovers of water sports can swim, sail, water ski, and scuba dive at places such as Falcon Lake in Whiteshell Provincial Park and Clear Lake in Riding Mountain National Park.

The Winnipeg Blue Bombers are a team in the Canadian Football League.

Anyone interested in fishing can take part in Flin Flon's Trout Festival. Riding Mountain National Park is home to wildlife such as black bear, moose, elk, deer, wolves, and bison. It is on a wooded section of the Manitoba **Escarpment**, 744 metres above the prairie. The escarpment has 36 hiking and riding trails through gorges, lakes, forests, and bogs. It also has golf facilities.

KEEP CONNECTED

The Manitoba Curling Association Bonspiel is one of the world's biggest curling competitions. To learn more about curling, visit **www.mycurling.com**.

The 1999 Pan-American Games attracted more than 5,000 athletes from 42 countries.

Manitoba has more golf courses per head than any other province.

Winnipeg hosted the Pan-American Games in 1967 and again in 1999. Excellent facilities were built for the games. Today, Winnipeg has an Olympic-sized swimming pool, which also houses the Aquatic Hall of Fame. It also has an indoor cycling track, a stadium, a track facility, and a rifle range. They are used by Manitoba's top athletes and by the general public for recreation.

GET THE FACTS

The World Championship Dog races take place at the Northern Manitoba Trappers' Festival in The Pas.

In 1981, Vicki Keith, from Winnipeg, swam across all five Great Lakes.

Winnipeg Beach is one of many beaches that Manitoba has to offer.

Manitoban Sylvia Burka competed internationally in two sports—speed skating and cycling. She won five national skating titles in the 1970s, and set a world record in cycling in 1982.

The National Frog Jumping Championships are the highlight of St. Pierre-Jolys Frog Follies.

CANADA

Canada is a vast nation, and each province and territory has its own unique features. This map shows important information about each of Canada's 10 provinces and three territories, including when they joined Confederation, their size, population, and capital city. For more information about Canada, visit **http://canada.gc.ca**.

Alberta
Entered Confederation: 1905
Capital: Edmonton
Area: 661,848 sq km
Population: 3,632,483

British Columbia
Entered Confederation: 1871
Capital: Victoria
Area: 944,735 sq km
Population: 4,419,974

Manitoba
Entered Confederation: 1870
Capital: Winnipeg
Area: 647,797 sq km
Population: 1,213,815

New Brunswick
Entered Confederation: 1867
Capital: Fredericton
Area: 72,908 sq km
Population: 748,319

Newfoundland and Labrador
Entered Confederation: 1949
Capital: St. John's
Area: 405,212 sq km
Population: 508,990

SYMBOLS OF MANITOBA

FLAG

COAT OF ARMS

FLOWER
Prairie Crocus

Map Labels

Alert

Baffin Bay

Baffin Island

Davis Strait

Iqaluit (Frobisher Bay)

Ivujivik

Labrador Sea

NEWFOUNDLAND

Schefferville

Happy Valley-Goose Bay

Island of Newfoundland

Chisasibi (Fort George)

Gander
Saint John's

QUEBEC

Sept-Iles

Gulf of St. Lawrence

St. Pierre and Miquelon (FRANCE)

Moosonee

Chibougamau

PRINCE EDWARD ISLAND

Sydney

Quebec

NEW BRUNSWICK

Charlottetown

Fredericton

Sherbrooke

Saint John

Halifax

Sudbury

Montreal

NOVA SCOTIA

Ottawa

Lake Huron

Lake Ontario

Toronto
Hamilton
London

Lake Erie

Hudson Bay

0   200   400 Kilometers
0   200   400 Miles

Species

BIRD
Great Grey Owl

TREE
White Spruce

ANIMAL
Bison

Northwest Territories
Entered Confederation: 1870
Capital: Yellowknife
Area: 1,346,106 sq km
Population: 42,940

Nova Scotia
Entered Confederation: 1867
Capital: Halifax
Area: 55,284 sq km
Population: 939,531

Nunavut
Entered Confederation: 1999
Capital: Iqaluit
Area: 2,093,190 sq km
Population: 531,556

Ontario
Entered Confederation: 1867
Capital: Toronto
Area: 1,076,395 sq km
Population: 12,986,857

Prince Edward Island
Entered Confederation: 1873
Capital: Charlottetown
Area: 5,660 sq km
Population: 140,402

Quebec
Entered Confederation: 1867
Capital: Quebec City
Area: 1,542,056 sq km
Population: 7,782,561

Saskatchewan
Entered Confederation: 1905
Capital: Regina
Area: 651,036 sq km
Population: 1,023,810

Yukon
Entered Confederation: 1898
Capital: Whitehorse
Area: 482,443 sq km
Population: 33,442

BRAIN TEASERS

Test your knowledge of Manitoba by trying to answer these boggling brain teasers!

1 True or False?

Winnipeg is the youngest city on the Prairies.

2 True or False?

Manitoba became a province on July 15, 1870.

3 Multiple Choice

What city was named for a character in a science fiction novel?
a) Winnipeg
b) Virden
c) Flin Flon
d) Brandon

4 True or False?

About 125,000 immigrants arrived from eastern Canada, Britain, and Europe between 1871 and 1891.

5 Make a Guess

Where in Manitoba are polar bears commonly found?

6 True or False?

The Pan American Games were held in Winnipeg in 1989.

7 Make a Guess

What is the name of the statue that stands on top of Manitoba's Legislative Building?

8 Multiple Choice

What event is held in Gimli each year?
a) Folklorama
b) Gimli Icelandic Festival
c) Canadian National Ukrainian Festival
d) the Mennonite Heritage Festival

1. False. It is the oldest city on the Prairies.   2. True.   3. C, Flin Flon was named after Professor Josiah Flintabbatey Flonatin, a character in a science fiction novel titled *The Sunless City* by E. Preston Muddock.   4. True.   5. Polar bears are commonly found in Churchill.   6. False. The games were held in 1999.   7. The name of the statue is the Golden Boy.   8. B, the Gimli Icelandic Festival is held in Gimli each year.

MORE INFORMATION

GLOSSARY

Canadian Shield: a region of ancient rock that encircles the Hudson Bay and covers part of mainland Canada

coniferous: evergreen trees with needles and cones

deciduous: trees or shrubs that shed leaves every year

escarpment: a steep slope or cliff

gristmill: a mill that grinds grain

Group of Seven: a group of Canadian painters, most famous for their paintings of Canadian landscape

hydroelectric: electricity generated by the power of water

hydrophone: an instrument that detects underwater sounds

junction: a place where railways or other pathways meet

mainstream: the common trend of opinion, art, or activity within a society

pavillions: buildings that house exhibitions

pemmican: dried meat that is pounded into a paste with melted fat

tributaries: streams that flow into larger streams or rivers

tundra: an Arctic or subarctic plain with a permanently frozen subsoil where mosses and lichens are the main types of vegetation

BOOK

Beckett, Harry. *Canada's Land and People: Manitoba*. Calgary: Weigl Educational Publishers Limited, 2008.

Foran, Jill. *Winnipeg: Gateway to the West*. From the Canadian Cities series. Calgary: Weigl Educational Publishers Limited, 2002.

Kissock, Heather. *Canadian Industries: Agriculture*. Calgary: Weigl Educational Publishers Limited, 2007.

Simon, Elizabeth. *Canadian Sites and Symbols: Manitoba*. Calgary: Weigl Educational Publishers Limited, 2004.

WEBSITES

Manitoba tourist information
http://travelmanitoba.com

The Government of Manitoba
www.gov.mb.ca

Manitoba Museum
www.manitobamuseum.ca

Some websites stay current longer than others. To find more Manitoba websites, use your Internet search engine to look up such topics as "Manitoba," "Winnipeg," "Prairie Provinces," or any other topic you want to research.

INDEX